Taylor Lautner

ABDO
Publishing Company

Big
Buddy BOOKS
Buddy Bios

by **Sarah Tieck**

VISIT US AT
www.abdopublishing.com

Published by ABDO Publishing Company, 8000 West 78th Street, Edina, Minnesota 55439.

Printed in the United States of America, North Mankato, Minnesota.
102010
012011

 PRINTED ON RECYCLED PAPER

Coordinating Series Editor: Rochelle Baltzer
Contributing Editors: Megan M. Gunderson, BreAnn Rumsch, Marcia Zappa
Graphic Design: Maria Hosley
Cover Photograph: *AP Photo*: Brad Weingarden/PictureGroup via AP IMAGES.
Interior Photographs/Illustrations: *AP Photo*: Vince Bucci/Fox/PictureGroup via AP IMAGES (p. 19), Jeff Daly/ PictureGroup via AP IMAGES (p. 27), Mark Davis/Hope for Haiti Now (p. 25), Peter Kramer/NBC NewsWire via AP Images (p. 21), Chris Pizzello (p. 4), Matt Sayles (pp. 17, 28), Adam Taylor/NBCU Photo Bank via AP Images (p. 23); *Getty Images*: Vince Bucci (p. 14), Barry King/WireImage (p. 7), Jon Kopaloff/FilmMagic (p. 13), J. Merritt/FilmMagic (p. 11), Albert L. Ortega/WireImage (p. 9), Sgranitz/WireImage (p. 11).

Library of Congress Cataloging-in-Publication Data

Tieck, Sarah, 1976-
 Taylor Lautner : star of Twilight / Sarah Tieck.
   p. cm. -- (Big buddy biographies)
  ISBN 978-1-61714-704-3
 1. Lautner, Taylor, 1992---Juvenile literature. 2. Actors--United States--Biography--Juvenile literature. I. Title.
 PN2287.L2855T54 2011
 791.4302'8092--dc22
  [B]
                        2010037882

Taylor
Lautner

Contents

Taylor plays Jacob Black in the Twilight movies.

Rising Star

Taylor Lautner is a talented actor. He has appeared in several popular movies. Taylor is best known for starring in the Twilight movie **series**.

5

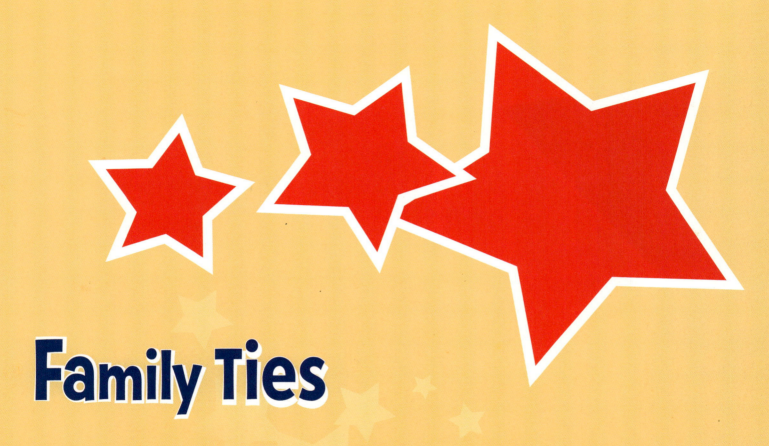

Family Ties

Taylor Daniel Lautner was born in Grand Rapids, Michigan, on February 11, 1992. Taylor's parents are Deborah and Daniel Lautner. He has a younger sister named Makena.

Sometimes Makena attends events with Taylor.

Taylor grew up in Hudsonville, Michigan. There, he attended Jamestown Elementary School. Taylor spent time with his family and friends. He enjoyed laughing, watching movies, and eating ice cream.

When Taylor was young, his dad was an airline pilot. His mom worked in an office.

Karate Kid

When Taylor was six, he began studying martial arts. Martial arts are Asian fighting arts, such as karate. They are often practiced as a sport.

People quickly noticed Taylor's skills. Soon, he was working with a teacher who was a world karate **champion**.

At about age eight, Taylor started traveling to worldwide **competitions**. Over the years, he won several championships!

Taylor has a black belt in karate! This means he is an expert. He can do moves such as flips and kicks.

Oregon

California

Nevada

PACIFIC OCEAN

Los Angeles

Arizona

M E X I C O

Starting Out

Taylor's karate coach encouraged him to **audition** for acting parts. Taylor found he enjoyed acting. In 2001, he became a **professional** actor. He got a part in the movie *Shadow Fury*.

Around 2003, the Lautner family moved to Los Angeles, California. Living there would make it easier for Taylor to find acting work.

In Los Angeles, Taylor had some small television parts. And, he attended events such as movie openings.

13

Did you know...

The Adventures of Sharkboy and Lavagirl 3-D is an action fantasy movie. The story is set on a pretend planet and the characters have special powers.

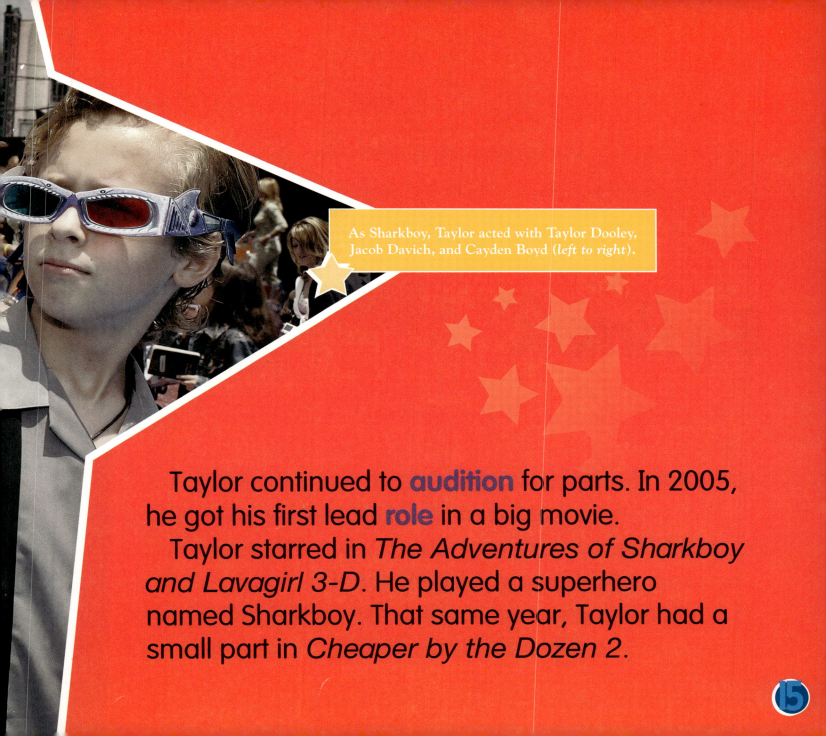

Taylor continued to **audition** for parts. In 2005, he got his first lead **role** in a big movie.

Taylor starred in *The Adventures of Sharkboy and Lavagirl 3-D*. He played a superhero named Sharkboy. That same year, Taylor had a small part in *Cheaper by the Dozen 2*.

Big Break

In 2008, Taylor played Jacob Black in the movie *Twilight*. This movie became very popular. It even won awards!

The movie is based on the first book in a **series** by author Stephenie Meyer. It is the story of a teenager named Bella and a vampire named Edward. Jacob is Bella's friend. He and Edward are enemies.

Robert Pattinson (*left*) plays Edward in the Twilight movies. Kristen Stewart (*center*) plays Bella. Robert, Kristen, and Taylor are friends offscreen.

Twilight was so popular that a second movie was planned. It is called *The Twilight Saga: New Moon*.

In the second movie, Jacob becomes a werewolf. Taylor needed to gain about 30 pounds (14 kg) for the part. Some people thought he could no longer play Jacob. But, Taylor worked out and ate a lot. So, he kept his part!

In 2010, Taylor won a Teen Choice Award for playing Jacob in *New Moon*.

A Working Actor

In 2009, *New Moon* was **released**. That year, Taylor also worked on the third movie in the **series**. *The Twilight Saga: Eclipse* was released in 2010.

The Twilight movies were so popular that Taylor became a well-known movie star! Now, reporters often **interview** him. And, stories and pictures of him appear in magazines and newspapers.

An Actor's Life

As an actor, Taylor spends time practicing lines. During filming, he works on a set for several hours each day.

Sometimes, Taylor travels to other states or countries to make movies. He may be away from home for a couple of months at a time.